# While We're Here

# While We're Here

Steven Henry Madoff

lingo books
Hard Press, Inc.
West Stockbridge, MA

Grateful acknowledgment to the editors of the *Michigan Quarterly Review*, *Bomb*, *Orion*, and *lingo* in which many of these poems appeared. The poem "Elements" first appeared in an earlier version in the exhibition catalogue *Outcasts: Catherine Lee*, published by the Lenbachhaus, Munich, Germany.

Cover Art: Detail from *Pallas Expelling the Vices from the Garden of Virtue*, Andrea Mantegna, 1502, collection of the Louvre, Paris, France. Credit: Erich Lessing/Art Resource, New York.
Cover design by Lloyd Ziff
Typeset by Chad Odefey
Published in the United States by
Hard Press, Inc.
a non-profit organization:
West Stockbridge, MA 01266
ISBN 1-889097-37-3

*for Pamela*

# Contents

## Us

They're intertwined, there, the one with the other,
     knowledge and hunger, the gold fruit on iron boughs
traced in the hardening light each season gathers.
     All day they've waited, the first ones, in the blue
of an unbroken sky. Because there are no words,
     no words are needed, or cloth, or the first weight
of promises. They've come to this, the new place, spurred
     by wind, waking, brought to the created seat
of earth, with its deep fragrance of braided atoms.
     They are waiting in the unexpected air,
in the unbroken light, and slowly find they've come
     to see what need is, watching as forms gather
meanings, so that the names must be spoken, as their
     tongues learn each other, to love the second day.
They're intertwined there, yes, the one with the other,
     knowledge and hunger, gold fruit on iron boughs.

# Part One

*A Mutation in the Air*

# Elements

Along the river, the metal is rushing,
   gun-metal
waters are falling and rising, higher and
higher. The sky is a torn scrim, light crashing
   through agate
clouds, and the slabs of dark pound the water, stand
down from ether. Everything is pliable,
changing. The sinuous streams of atoms plait

and separate and charge. Matter, involute
   and teeming,
renews itself, re-forms from the spoiling heath,
the brackish tidepool, the smelted silicates,
   transistors,
poles and flows, energy, information, paths.
Rising and falling, the breaking sky framing
the pounding light, and the metal plummets or

resists, which is the way things live. *Even then*
   *I felt gleams*
*like flashings of a shield—the earth and common*
*face of Nature spake rememberable things....*
   Language
itself a machine of nature. Breath, dipthongs,
vowel clusters, speaking. The blocks of phonemes
sliding into place, bearing the carriage

of thought, making the shapes known and unfearful
   as the eye

travels, sweeping the trees bending. Points of dew
like muons in single streams or strings of pearls
   refracting.
Each small dome a shifting globe. Or an I who
builds itself by containing consciously
the changing light of rememberable things.

# Fishing

Crouching to it then, I smelled the sweet rankness
of soil combusting in a field of sumac.
     Elms rising under milk densities of light.
Sunlit glare fanning out. A hill of opaque
     splendor done in frost. Jutting limestone and weight-
       less branches dark against the white sun's richness.


     And there were other things. The chill-water pools
of light-drenched plankton spinning, schooling minnows
       racing in a pocket of oxygen. Toad-
stools, toads, gnats, fleas, spider, worm, the mired slough,
     a milk snake's flaking slough, ovenbirds, bluebirds,
       fruitless plane trees. Here was the limitless spool


     of generation. Or so it seemed then, crouch-
ing as the light turned blue, blue-gray, and sounds fell
       closer to the earth. The low report of things
moving unseen, changing for the nightly chill.
     Or simply because being wanted something,
       something else. The minnows darting out of reach,

as the hook goes down, again down, down again....

## Diana and Actaeon

A cloud of flies

eats at the wounds
clotting. The dead game's gore is shining its bruised light.
Below, a valley thick
with resinous cypress,
awl-shaped leaves rising like narrow crowns
in crowded peaks, the straight trunks close, as sound
echoes along the stones
glinting. Beryl, calcites,
bladed gypsum, cat's eye, stilbite sheaves, a druse
of rose quartz black

till sunlight hits
its bluish vein in a cave's wall carved by water.
The soft scrape of his foot
is racing where he's drawn
to the cave's mouth, its arch by a wide pool.
She's bathing with her women: classical,
the one pure militant
for the Untouched. Her wet
skin is white, muscles coiled. The way she looks, she looks
like him, killer

of boar, stags, bear.
Her mouth opens as he moves. She turns as his eyes
find her, the once unseen,
her arrows out of reach.
And the women shout. They're startled to see

a man here, in the yellow air, frozen,
    like a deer strayed, unsure,
caught in an open patch
of light on its blameless flank before it flees.
    Now, suddenly,

    he wears the lean
mark of the chosen, taken by Mystery to
satisfy principle.
    "Go ahead," she says. "Try
to say how you, how you saw me like this"—
then flings the water that changes him. It loosens
    form. His ears pointed, toes
hoof. His neck starts to swell.
A tan pelt sprouts in tufts from his ankle, a wrist,
    his shrinking knee.

    And his dogs tear,
drag him twisting through the sedge and rocks as he tries
to speak, cry each dog's name,
    cry, "No! I'm Actaeon,
Actaeon!" The name his friends called, wishing
he could have seen the great stag fall, bleeding
    on the damp, flowered floor
of nightshade, lady's thumb,
a fire of pinks. Even the mud had its light-
    confirming sheen.

# The Shapes

It happens slowly, the clouds traveling
    at different speeds,
the slipping sounds of wind
on the bladed leaves of sweetgum,
      the light later,
the brown trout, the smallmouth bass
    rising, you can see them
rising up through the water,
and fox sparrows down in the leaves, warbling.
Slowly something bends,
    and something feeds
a limestone stream, easing bleared ice,

the listing axis trued to an old house
in the mild ascent
    of stars and weather. Reeds,
the freed vowels of crocuses,
      the sticking curls
of fiddleheads, the egg sacs
    held milky and viscous
in a twig's joint of laurel
and dust. The slow and unbidden process.
Oracle of seed,
      still expectant,
green and turning among the rocks.

# Mycelia

Now they come,
rising from damp whorled cones of cedar, cypress,
from dank soil, needled earth, ant kingdom,
corbelled underworld of roots. Jack o' lantern,
    chanterelles,
or here, thick boletes and velvet blue spread's waste,
or the terrifying amanita, spurned
    and lethal.

Did they seem
so mild? They induced visions, death when swallowed.
Others smelled of apricot, with a look claimed
by flesh in the gray afterlight of autumn.
    When you held
them, their veined weight, waxy and slick, was swollen,
puffed like scaly, impossible eggs, their slime
    soft as mud.

Spores explode
from splash cups or devil's urns, and some migrate
differently, the molds, dough-white or crusted.
They drink until a bursting wall breeds the tubes
    called *hyphae*
that flow with proteins, water, carbohydrates,
oils, and bear their motile, sensing astrolabe
    for fungi—

the gametes,
which are sex cells that orient each hypha

toward its moon or sun, so they knit the threads
that fuse a mushroom's fruiting body. Some shed
    abortive
veils like doctors' gauze and rise in taffeta,
dead drunk at the ball, their flesh as pale as blood
    additive.

## A Mutation In the Air

Along the light, the shapes were shifting again.
    The butterworts
on leafless stalks writhing in a boil of flies.
The white stems of phlox, the lobed petals wilting
    in the August
heat that fell. And there, the long blue sky that bleeds
to gentian, it deepened in the screen's quartz-
tuned intensity as it flipped through elapsed

time, so that time's shape was also changed, was freed.
    Here, speeding streams
and waterfalls slowed to stationary blasts
and slow clouds leaned like mountains that seemed to stride.
    There were high clouds
gliding, rising through the stained pixels' mists
to claim their voluntary power. The spumes
and cataracts gave way to cleaving slate beds.

The sky was turning, breaking. And the seasons
    were running on,
eager for this, the end of the century.
And then? Do the meanings fade? Are they gone then
    or just unchained—
the shapes rising up, above the marsh, snow
geese slanting, first dark then white, where the clouds bend
and race and look like men, like leaning mountains,

but are only chance mutations in the air.
    What could have been

and what is, do they erode as the scene shifts?
Or are they like fire? The way it quivers
    in freeze-frame and
shows, even here, what nature is: not grafted,
but force driven through. (The long shapes were shifting
again, backwards now. Wilting petals stiffen.)

# Part Two

*After Nature*

# On the Banks

It happens slowly, the clouds traveling
at different speeds,
    the slipping sounds of wind
in the gathered leaves, campfires,
      the light later,
the brown trout, the smallmouth bass
   rising to the lures,
rising up through the water,
and the pale thatched huts on the banks, rising
by the river's bend.
      Boys in the woods,
sparrows flying up, laughter, cries

in the trees, and the settling of loose
shadows in the spent,
   late afternoons after seed
planting. By the small pearl-gray spring,
     kneeling, a girl
drinks from a cup. A plain space
   is set out for dancing,
for the prayers to appeal
to the gods of earth, of thunder. And this
is what is found: beads,
    an amulet
under the village, the first place.

# Pallas Expelling the Vices from the Garden of Virtue

All of them have come.
They've gathered, it seems, because they're the half-formed
and what is in them is terrible:
deceit, sloth, greed, even Venus, the goddess of love,
     is terrible because she rides on the centaur's back,
  taken as a form
of chaos—as passion is always fugitive.
Half beasts, half humans, wading in scum
and lilies, the hard-eyed ones, did they think they'd settled,
     or was it a need to smell roses without a thick-

  ness of soot and dream
of mist, a slow moon, heaven under stars? Or
was it theirs once, too, this level world?
Or no, that the villages and taverns, the walled cities
     were not enough. So they came, avid, to the first place.
    Still, what matters are
the true signs. How Ignorance is crowned. The monkey
with a woman's breast who carries crimes
in purses. The ones who are allegories, but are al-
    so real. How the armless girl, the one called Idleness,

  hauled on a short leash,
has opiated eyes, stares dead on, as if
she knows me for what I am. Today,
at lunch, we saw a woman like her, a young addict
     who tried to eat. She was nodding off, fork in mid-air,
  in a plane above.
Did it seem like Paradise? First the needle's prick,

then nothing, not even hunger, which
drove her there only to find that in the bright noon's haze,
       it isn't right to be two things. A bay tree that bears

    breasts, belly, arms, legs
can't run to a lover. A bearded satyr,
horned, with human hands. Or Pallas, whose
spear is broken off, signifying triumph, and shows
       that Paradise is only saved by armed rebellion.
    Her blouse a mixture
of gold pigment and arsenic. In the canvas,
half-way up, under a monstrous, frag-
mentary cliff, there's a latticed hedge, pinkish roses
       settled in by an arbor of apples, pale lemons

    now peaceful against
gathering skies—which no one's even noticed.
Not one fruit has been touched. It's an old
story. In the Garden of Virtue, there is no need
       for hunger. It's only on the other side the theme
    of want gets practiced.
And here, how it tells, how the picture's time is made:
a time is ending, its present tense
is past. Meanwhile, you can see them, the same vices—willed,
       pale, entering the world. All that time, we were waiting.

# Game

A forest floor. The dense sounds: a boot or hoof.
The sluice over iced stone,
        its light slanting,
    scraping elderberry. Her head, bland as turf,
    halts, missed in the shadowed screen
the grove's changing
light amends. The light is coming to its end,
gone into the firs, the pines.
        Still, their eyes swerve,
    grown used to nature, up, down, searching the bent
    needles for a sign that gleans
a tuft of fur
on a branchlet in dark hours. Now she moves,
a sound filled with the immense
        longing the damned
    know well, heard in the four-by-four: pounding hooves,
    brush whiplashed, the sense of chance
unwinding, tamed
by power in their eyes as they find her terse
breath pluming in a searchbeam.
        Is it always
    like this? On an earth without mercy. Small force
    against small force. And to claim
this only: a
foothold for an instant before the blue Earth
falls away. She runs. And they
        break the branch screen,
    down on foot, barrels up, waiting an eased birth,
    the satisfying bead by

the right craftsman.
They close the route in briar. Her once shifting
course is clear, it's like a chain—
      her muzzle broad,
    now dropped. The wet glint, the weight, the game wafting,
    as the blunt hide is dragged, then
thrown on the hood.

# The City

She's dreaming in the air. The night is clear.
The building rises where it shouldn't be,
where groves were once that lit each rite.
A red light and a green light waking there.
She lifts her fork. It's scented pleasantly
and drifts into the beams that beat.
Her eyes are closed. A shirt, moon lit, hovers
in the air. She's dreaming in the
night, who's lost her taste for animals, though
not for men. The building rises where her
eyes turn bright, green then red. She bites.

# They Travel

They travel in lines, in great rows, with lights
turned on as a red sun lowers behind cooling towers.
They come from distances, from homes in even lots,
ornaments of wrought iron, azaleas in mannered beds,
the satellite dishes, the cars, the intricate routes
    to brick schools, to their first boyfriends, to seats
    in darkened theaters. The fields are cleared of unkempt powers,
    thistle, bramble, the wandering green snake, lance-leaved goldenrod.
    Macadam, the alleys behind backs of houses that
    spread in numbered patterns, that are seen from the heights
of airplanes, down on the cars that travel
over cloverleafs, through the ex-urban grid, and out then
off the Interstate to edge through vast acreage
to parking lots laid out like parcels. They walk together, their
conversations small, planning meeting points for later.
    Now they're entering. Massive paddlewheels
    churn water. The atrium holds palm trees—its oxygen
    is purified. The sky is empty. It's like a backdrop cleared
    to focus on the players. *America. Winter*
    *Garden. Cross County. The Willows* or *Heritage.*
The tiers are filled with music. Teenage boys
wearing clown suits call to beckon strangers. And a swooning
sense of marvel. Shops with antlers on the walls with
videos of waterways and pines. Hope chests of Brazilian
wood. The international food stalls. The cameras
    swiveling overhead to watch as they
    move among the credit-card-size calculators, the rings,
    mylar vests, the remote devices—watch as they leave again
    in rows, homeward, back from artificial paradise.
    It's night. Everywhere, light breathes their shining will.

## And Then

And after, what then?
Will they be like us? With beams and fiberoptics
tying them together soundlessly—unless
    it's a sound they want.
    And what will they glean
from nature? Ways to transport their forms? To release
even the body itself, so the flesh walks
    invisibly and
    time is a distance—
as the land was for us before our cars and flight—
that is swallowed. And death, will it be allowed?
    Chosen or refused?
    Only lenience
for the least populated regions, where they lead
lives of uproarious pleasure in the great
    domed cities, the closed
    ones under towers
arcing lucent rays of a virtual red sun.
Thus will it be settled. The last cyclones tamed.
    The weather, the growth
    of each plant lowered
to graceful cycles. For them, the newly redeemed,
floating in bright, harmonious spheres that sing
    above the green Earth.
    Or will it still be
like this? The same dark. The same flowers—indian
grass, horse balm—crushed under hooves as the deer runs.
    The cities unleashed,
    spread out to the gray

horizon. The riot's unrest played back again
and again. And the woman's hand. Her hand
    waiting, still outstretched.
    What will it contain?
In the raw seasons. As you learned the possible
truth. About history. The tribes and armies
    rushing over plains.
    A child who listened,
dreaming, in the middle of our century,
at a wooden desk. And who now must riddle
    what the stories mean.

# Part Three
*History*

# Germania

They rode their horses straight ahead.
For them it was no sin to offer a human sacrifice.
Was it the lame they offered? A boy of the enemy?
Or a captive soldier, tied to a post and killed standing up?
Offered to Mercury, the god they praised above all.
The young men asked for spears stained with blood, and had no taste for peace.
Like their fathers before them, who drank beer from a wooden cup
and would gamble even themselves, drunk, into slavery.
Clerics told them what horses heard
from the gods—either omens of war or their skills
at business. Sometimes at war
their women stood alongside in an open field or the woods,
begging their men to win, not live enslaved or beholden.
The moon above held aloft by a breath or strung from a rope.
"Why should we live by the sweat of our brows," they said,
"what we can get fast enough, faster, by a little loss of blood?"
They were good with short narrow spears called *frameae* thrust from the hip
or thrown, but preferred javelins rained down from a distance.
Their food was plain: fresh game, then cur-
dled milk and wild fruit. And went around in the matted
cloaks they fastened with a brooch or,
failing that, a thorn. Their tribes, as I record here, had the names
Usipi, the Chatti and Tencteri, flush by the Rhine,
and spreading out, the Bructeri, the Fosi, the Cherusci,
called "lazy fools," and the Aestii, who loved crude amber.
The peoples of Germany, with their reddish hair and big frames,
their fierce-looking blue eyes, it's true they never intermarried
with other races. The coasts were dismal, and the ocean
gray and limitless. So they were
poor and violent. And each day they lived, their blood was pure.

# Invention

"Progress, like the stars," he said,
"lights us. Like engines climbing, hungering fuels.
Their machines angelic and hopeful
metaphysically." The light was burning down
a low gray hill in a bramble of bindweed.
"And so," he said, "that early miracle, the wheel.
A practical solution to the burden
of the animal. How made?
From stone. But when we found a way, turning wood
and forge-blasting rims of iron willed
to navigate the holy circle, our symbol
of complete devotion"—here he made the sign
of the Cross, looked up and smiled
at me—"we found the round wheel, spoked and all, could
travel like the sun. So it was. God's will."
The light was almost gone. Bed
of earth, darkness. And now the fire slowly schooled
our eyes as he leaned closer, watchful
of his pupil. "This other purpose summons
clemency. Grace for wandering souls," he said.
"They learn the right direction from our compass wheel."
And turned to one alone. Blood
on his wrists, face, his burned side, ankles
where ropes tied him to the spokes and the small bone
broke through. "This is progress too," my master said.
"To think of them, souls rising. It's a way. All
faith asks is forgiveness, good.
Now look." There was a light brimming, full
in the dying eyes, *full*. And I knew it then,
why the everlasting wheel was invented.

# Diderot

The earth is whole, unwounded, it hears itself
　　　being, not by miracle but by mechanism,
　　going on in its shapeliness, which is merciless and free.
　　　　　—But if there is a God.
"But I may doubt it," he says.
　　　And there is no providence. No divine design.


Men are substance.—But is His Son? Is the gulf
　　　between the Son and us? Or is this essence-schism
　　between them, between the sheer Father and the one progeny,
　　　　　in spirit subtracted,
so that He is a thought *red*
　　and the Son is the heat there, a flame, the made-known?


And then there is this, the earthquake of Lisbon,
　　　1755. How can a streaming grace hold?
　　The one who is Unknowingness, the light who is One-In-Three,
　　　　　He's sentenced to life then,
called in the Paris cafés
　　　to flesh, called "Mr. Being," His priests not the bright tongue


of Mystery, but landholders, rings of pain.
　　　"If there are a thousand souls damned for every soul
　　saved," he writes, "then the Devil wins the argument, doesn't he?
　　　　　And without abandon-
ing his Son to death."—But say
　　　He is not abandoned. Say He is descent, wing


45

of Him, invisible, the Word now matter,
>>so that matter can read His likeness and become, through
>grace, *with* Him. No, we have too much cruelty and disorder
>>for a Divine Mechanick.
And then there's this, that science
>>doesn't need Him to read nature's breathing engine

feeding on itself. And suppose.... But the Church
>>finds "suppose" inflaming. This is the *kerygma*. The
>Trinity is Him revealed. A shape defined in the bright whir,
>>transparency, fabric
of faith's water. In Vincennes
>>he's held in prison. His early works are taken,

burned. He charts his grand encyclopedia,
>>which replaces faith with reason, *is* faith. And released,
>he continues. "The Christian religion is to my
>>mind the most absurd and
atrocious in dogmas:
>>the most unintelligible and entangled,

subject to divisions, sects, heresies;
>>the most dangerous to sovereigns, its bad abuse,
>its discipline; most flat, Gothic, gloomy in ceremonies;
>>still the most puerile and
unsociable in its
>>morality; the most intolerant of all."

—The Spirit is like breath, it's on the Word of
>>the Father. It carries Him, a light. Yet in *Rameau's
Nephew*, belief is nothing. We contradict, are contradiction.
>>And he, though not the end,
in 1765:
>>"I've never seen that long file of priests, acolytes

in white albs strewing flowers, and the crowd of
men following in religious silence, they who
fall prostrate on these cool stones, and never heard that grave chant sung
and answered by children
without being stirred in my
inmost heart, without tears flowing, here, from my eyes."

# Germania

It's what they take from Tacitus, climbing up
the sweeping marble stairs done in Roman
style. They light the candles. The sun has slipped.
The year is 1939. They've been
sitting late, and still in uniform, to reimagine
history, how a rising genus fits
their genealogy. Not Tacitus's, but Berlin's.
The sun comes up. They keep their candles lit.

# In Bosnia

"Everything was on fire,
    and we saw them throwing bodies into the flames."
  There are 200,000 deaths. There are 12,000 in the city alone,
      and winter is coming.
The exploding shells are everywhere. People sprawl on mattresses
in basements, stairwells, woodsheds and garages, anywhere protected.
      The cleric is crying. "Is it because we are Muslims?
  Is it because we are Muslims?"

"If the Christians were massacred
    like Muslims are being killed here, then Muslims
  would be condemned as mad Fundamentalists. And we have no one to lean on.
      With the winter coming.
No, we are the new Jews of Europe." There is still fresh meat, but prices,
in German marks, have gone so high, so that now the people can't be fed.
      And instead, smuggled Serbian cigarettes, shoes, costume
jewelry, comic books, old films

are sold out at the flea markets
    to people who lack staples, even flour.
  A kilo of wheat is worth three times more than a gram of gold. And there isn't wood
      enough, not wood to make
enough proper coffins. In Teocak, local Croats and Muslims
are still fighting side by side. But in Fojnica, Father Miletic says
      the Croats are the "big losers in this war." This is where
  they came, the four Muslim soldiers,

shouting in the courtyard, "Halt! Put
    your hands up!" And Father Milicevic, near

to one of them, said there were no weapons in the monastery. Then one shoved
                    his gun into the back
of Brother Nikica, screaming "I'm going to kill you!" And to him
the Brother said, "Then kill," and the man discharged his weapon. The bullets
                    also killed Father Milicevic. And then the Father
        Migic, standing there, was injured.


So the gunman put two more shots
            in the back of his head. Then the soldiers left
        the monastery. Which circle of Hell is this? On an earth without mercy.
                Is it Ugolino,
whose teeth gnaw the skull of Archbishop Ruggieri, or the
trees whose sap is steaming blood bleeding from the torn branches, crying out,
                    there, in the ancient woods of Europe. So that the falling
        leaves are no different here, in


Stupni Do, when trucks on the dirt
            road come up so suddenly, through the deep shafts
        of the valley, in mid-afternoon light. They are still outside, before the snow
                begins. The potatoes,
squash, and beets still being gathered when the first shouts cry up, and now they
run, the woodlands up ahead. A glove is dropped, jackets and cigarettes,
                    shoes in the muddy paths, a doll. But they are caught, falling,
        or at home. In the afternoon


they are hiding here, a crawl space
            where they, the three women, are shot in the face,
        holding each other's arms, one's throat cut, and there, the two sisters, Amela and
                Suvada Likic, they
are 19 and 22, dragged out, raped and burned. A boy burned, naked,
one foot in an old army boot, the fingers of one hand chopped off. The
                Croats are shouting for them to lie down, the man on top
        of the small boy and the mother

beside them, then stabbed, then the shots
   to the head. Burned. A girl is ten years old whose
  skull is smashed. Six pyres are built and the bodies thrown on all night, the low scent
        of roaring flesh, yellow
leaves rising. "Everything was on fire, and we saw the naked
bodies thrown into the flames." "We are being scattered like fallen leaves,"
        the cleric says. "Survive in a reservation to chop
  wood, the few of us left to work

their gardens." Out of nothing, earth,
    the skies and waters, seeds for planting, and the
  brightness of mountains. Rain and the sound of birds calling in the trees, the deep light.
        Now all of them have come.
And what is in them is terrible. The streets are littered with glass and
debris torn from buildings by exploding shells. In Banja Luka, the
        mosques are burned. "Don't you wish you were a Serb," the waiter said.
  "We have the finest army in

Europe. Finest. With what we're worth,
    we could make it all the way to Vienna."
 ˙ Her 11-year-old brother, Sanel, died then in the Serb bombardment late
        last year, but it's not him
she speaks of, Sabina, at the kitchen table. Seven years old and
saying, "Look, here's my mortar shell. My father found it. And look, here's my
        turtle. His name is Peti. I found him," Sabina said.
"Yes. I found him in the garden."

# Century

A boy is running beside a train in Germany, as the tined tracks,
forking off, curve into the regions of summer. To the left, the track

is a fading mystery. He thinks he has never gone there. The right
track hooks through gathering woodlands, primrose and fireweed, blinding sheets

of juniper, through which he saw once the white, blurred sock of a stag's leg.
Then his father said, *Freies Geleit.*
                    The first cars shift, windows blank, flecked

with shapes caught, then loosened on the panes. He starts to run. The gravel breaks,
shrapnel shooting from the wheels. The boy is taken, swept by the oblique

pleasures of watching travel under way, or the one word, *verheißung,*
promise, spoken again. The rooted families, lone fathers, boyfriends

wave from the platform. And summer has a voice that calls now in the small
gusts of heat built and pumped, a flushing sound of hoarse air drumming crenel-

lated iron.
        It is morning. In the light, the deep smell of moistened
well stones, like sweetness rotting or a sump, bleeds into the rising blend

of gasoline and dust. He runs, and there are dark pools merged with shadows
in the vines, burned newspaper, stone, flying leaves in the lucent shallows

of channeled railbeds. The platform empties, falls into Sunday stillness,
which he has left... for what? To watch them as they settle into places?

The low, excited conversations? And knowing the familiar gone,
if only to return to later? But something else. Is it the un-

said, the not-learned-yet, the unconjugated past with its sound like wheels
caught, or the trains themselves? The *under* of it, the unequivocal

no seeping up through brightness, like hairline cracks in porcelain.
And then the train, with sudden concentration, seems to gather force, run-

ing out along the lines, in the warming glare of summer, the pure light.
It is all for him, still, the sheerest pleasure. The air, white delicate

flowers, the ones called thimbleweed, and he runs. The train is out of sight.
*Freies Geleit*, his father says. Which means safe conduct. *Freies Geleit*.

# Part Four
*While We're Here*

# Second

Listen. There's something I want to tell you—

what I knew when I started.
Not the sounds of crowds roaring, or a gun.
Not even an angle of starlight.
Bodies in fields had been covered for centuries.
Sycamores grew there, under the red sun
falling. They were waiting, the still strange properties,

and we were still to meet. After that,
our years. How we flirted

by a river, talking late,
as the others passed on a summer night.
But not yet. I'll tell you what I knew:
already it wasn't easy being second.
Yes, of course, I saw it even then that

there are seconds, thirds. That it's hardly uncommon.
And it's true how it's necessary:
on earth, to keep the planet

filled, you need workers to move
things. The ones who play what the others write.
Ladies in waiting. The retinues
in blue damask and yellow stockings who are meek

and learned long ago, harshly, that a seat
of power means it rests on someone else's back.

I knew it's full of us, history.
Men with muskets in a grove

who fall in bursts of powder.
Or simply, in my case, to be born in
Cancer, the crab going sideways on

land, in water, a bad sign of indirectness,
under the father's gaze. To be the son
born after the daughter. Who at first seems a plus,
but is always under suspicion
because of this discomfort—

that the boy doesn't look him
in the face. It's only that for us, for

seconds, we know it, what our shapes
are meant for: to hold the part that was left over.
So we're always looking, as I was for
you, to find the small wholeness of our measure
by what fills us, like a window op-
ened onto a scent of thyme

that changes everything—

sight, the taste of oranges, what you said.
What I learned after, I learned from you.
So that I can bear to think of them, the fair ones,
and father, whose hardness is repeated,
because they're above, all of them, stars shining down.
Their brilliant light. Ungraspably.
Yes, and their hard light, shining.

# A Kind of Work

There was a god-shaped hole, was calling, calling.
A trying-to-find-itself, and naturally dark.
Where had I come from to find it, through the lean darkness,
to enter? Was it bad to need an I, to live

in the blowing suit of flesh? And the calling
god-shaped hole, I found it not a place, no, not a place
to look through, or a scent, but a broken kind of work
I came to, once exhausted, in a kind of grove—

a blunt site with a sound, imploring, kneeling—
and freshened myself by asking, loosening the hooks
of air, of white-tooled water, the taste of you, the crease
of light that held time, so that I could abide, live,

so that only then was I a part of the weave....

## Shirt

In the dream it was high up, fluttering, dark,
darker than the corner, and somehow glinting.
A bat, I thought. Was I in the barn in Maine?
And where was our bedside racquet, our half-blind,
nightlong backhand? Was she here, then, dreaming too?
Odd, this old comfort, this longing mixed with fear
so palpable and winged. Wrong. And still it hung
and dipped, velocity, ease, hovering, free....

Finally, from car light and street light, I made
its shape into a thing I knew, knew well, made
straight of cloth: the day's shirt dream-limp, left hanging,
swept side to side my ceiling's cloud-lit moon white.
The closet door was wide. It was beating still,
high up, deft and fleet and natural, I thought,
for so elegant a thing: my weightless gray,
my buttons' moon-gray glint, waiting to be touched.

# Wanting

Having come this far, there was
    from the start
        the hook inside you whose eye swivels,
    whose flung line is played and pulls you, and which is
    named now—this drawing-to
               with its weight—to ease it.

In the field whose one deer has
    turned, whose light's
        fallen, the grass and flowerfire call
and want their morning, their green eventfulness.
    They too, in their own way,
              are longing in the slate

light, in what is left, for that
    turning: heat
        again, something unequivocal
in the wind's coming lift and moistened sweetness.
    It calls to you, smells you
             on its hunt for blood, as

the hunter loves his target,
    his sweet meat,
        meat for wanting—it's that physical.
Or how, like singing up through climbing octaves,
    the meat can fall away
             to the unbodied gaze

of yearning. Sometimes like that
　　you learn it:
　　　　　how wanting is not the possible,
　　but affirms what you imagine, luminous
　　　　and rising in the blue
　　　　　　　air of dreaming. Or this:

that wanting is the weight that
　　burns, how it
　　　　　plunges, dissolving measure, equals
　　blindness, as it was when I loved her first, whose
　　　　goodness made me want my
　　　　　　　own, so that goodness was

an urgency, a magnet,
　　like a gate
　　　　　opened, drawing me to a source, pulled
　　there through the tunnel of everything else—as
　　　　wanting will, whether slow
　　　　　　　or racing, about ease

or money, things here, or what
　　god you wait
　　　　　for as the light falls inside you, full
　　of *last*. And as it hunts and smells your course, as
　　　　its line to tie snares you
　　　　　　　in its knots and catches,

you pull, pull it back to seize
　　its hunger,
　　　　　its day-after-day, and master, reel
　　it in, as want is the given urge in us
　　　　to make the partial tie
　　　　　　　a knot with wholeness. It's

what it's like in the late grass
    as it starts

          again. The light-dilated air, swelled
   weight of green... the being-field opening. This
      small urge in things. It's a

         kind of song, you hear it:

                *wanting.*

# The Changing Light

Now the light was changing time,
and each thing was changed, unheard.
  The Veracruz Man, with his one arm broken.
    The table, done in zinc, that bore
each acid stain, even the print of a hand.
  Light was streaming.

There was something there—a seam
in the failing clouds, the parts
  of air climbing,
    white with chutes of snow, the ice-scarred
river—something settled once, that once had been,
  now shifting, easing and breaking under strain.

It's not hard. You can see it,
what holds—even a small thing—
  because it stays still, as if nonbeing,
    somehow, can't enter the scaled well
of matter, so it turns away. And now, in
  the tilting light,

I sensed it, how the habits
were falling under, falling
  into the bright
    plane of change. Here, the now unsealed,
the *open*. And what rose from this, the sudden
flash of space, was a cleanliness unwinding

in the air, as if the light
of rememberable things
    had purged what it contained and then unburdened
        there, shaking and loosening, free
to reinvent, so that I was also free
    to loosen and

revise. That's how I knew that
even the smallest of things
    can change the bend,
        the arc of sight. And how tiny
the self is. Unbent. Easing. Now seeing suddenly
    that the father, in his way, was innocent.

## While We're Here

A boat on the river leaves no wake.
      The water, patient.
The sky here is white; the sun oblique.
      Miles away, the half arc
      of a bridge is like a pencil mark.
      A smudge of silence.

And closer, though it is still unheard,
      a plane no bigger
than a fly seems caught—as if a third
      element between sky
      and the small island, with its shadow.
      A long sigh of gears

shifts. Cars in a blue parcel of light
      are drawn to their one
purpose. And there, below in the streets,
      a boy running, figures,
      the couples moving in slow measure,
      doors flashing open.

And now, how it seems that each thing's weighed,
      here, just as it is—
as it is with us. The milkish light
      pouring. Pistil, stamen
      of the arched day lily, half open.
      The door as it was,

still ajar. A dense odor of earth,
      of another time
tilted to the axis of summer.
     And around us, being
seems to glide like the sun, look! pausing,
      filling, a bright gleam

moving on. My hands where your hands were.
     Here. Now. Suddenly
gleaming, all of it opening. Air.
    Lips. The better angel
    of my being called, it seems. Yes, called
    to honor you.

# Notes

"Elements": The quote, altered slightly, in italics, is from William Wordsworth, "Two-Part Prelude," lines 415-418, 1799.

"A Mutation in the Air": The poem alludes to Wordsworth's "Two-Part Prelude," lines 81-129, in the passage about rowing towards the huge cliff that upreared its head. The phrase "voluntary power" originates here.

"Pallas Expelling the Vices from the Garden of Virtue": The poem is based on the painting by Andrea Mantegna, done circa 1499-1502, in the collection of the Musée du Louvre, Paris.

"Germania": Tacitus, the Roman historian who lived from circa a.d. 56-115, wrote *Germania* in a.d. 98. All of the poem is taken from details of Tacitus's account. In the introduction to the Penguin Classics edition, 1973, H. Mattingly notes that the Nazis used Tacitus's little volume to construct the genealogy of the pure Arian breed.

"Diderot": References to Diderot are from *The Story of Civilization: Part IX, The Age of Voltaire* by Will and Ariel Durant, Simon and Schuster, New York, 1965. Diderot's quotes have been altered slightly to fit the scheme of the poem. Questions concerning Christian faith are based on *A History of God* by Karen Armstrong, Alfred A. Knopf, New York, 1993.

"In Bosnia": The poem is based on reporting in the *New York Times* on the war in Bosnia and Herzegovina. The journalists are John Kifner, Chuck Sudetic, and John F. Burns. All of the quotes have been altered slightly. The two main accounts, the slayings at the Franciscan monastery in Fojnica and the massacre in Stupni Do are by, respectively: Chuck Sudetic, "Killings in Bosnian Monastery Widen Croat-Muslim Divide," Friday, December 31, 1993; John F. Burns, "U.N.'s Grim Documentation at a Massacre Site in Bosnia," Thursday, October 28, 1993.

Photo: Susan Salinger

Steven Henry Madoff was born in New York City and educated at Columbia University, where he was the recipient of the Academy of American Poets Poetry Prize and was the editor of the *Columbia Review*. He went on to do his graduate work on a fellowship in literature at Stanford University. His art criticism has been published widely and translated into many languages. He was the executive editor of *ARTnews* magazine from 1987-1994 and in 1997 published *Pop Art: A Critical History* with University of California Press. He is the executive editor of *Joe*. He lives in South Salem, New York, with his wife and two children.